Smelly Old History
Medieval Muck

Mary Dobson

OXFORD UNIVERSITY PRESS

Oxford University Press, Great Clarendon Street, Oxford OX2 6DP

Oxford New York
Athens Auckland Bangkok Bogotá Buenos Aires Calcutta
Cape Town Chennai Dar es Salaam Delhi Florence Hong Kong Istanbul
Karachi Kuala Lumpur Madrid Melbourne Mexico City Mumbai
Nairobi Paris São Paulo Singapore Taipei Tokyo Toronto Warsaw
and associated companies in Berlin Ibadan

Oxford is a registered trade mark of Oxford University Press

Published in the United States
by Oxford University Press Inc., New York

© Mary Dobson 1998
The moral rights of the author have been asserted
First published 1998

Artwork: Vince Reid. Photographs: p.7 Weald and Downland Open Air
Museum, Sussex photo Stephen Oliver; p.22 London Dungeon.

British Library Cataloguing in Publication Data available

ISBN 0 19 910528 6

1 3 5 7 9 10 8 6 4 2

Printed in Great Britain

Contents

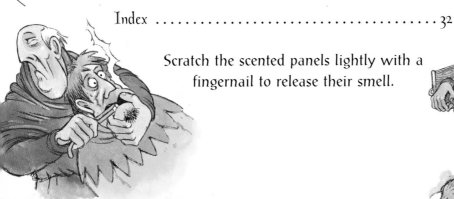

Scratch the scented panels lightly with a
fingernail to release their smell.

Sense of the Past

Life in medieval times could be really gripping. Imagine being a dashing knight in shining armour, or a beautiful lady in silken robes. Imagine the thrill of living in a brand new castle or taking a trip to the Holy Land. But before you get carried away, think again! Lurking in the depths of the castles were deadly dungeons and disgusting stenches. The penniless peasants, the kings, queens, nobles, and even the monks, had some pretty foul habits. Of course, the black rats had a great time wallowing in those stinking medieval muckheaps. But they, too, came to a sticky end!

Of all the senses of the past, we often forget the sense of smell! This book takes you on a tour of the mucky medieval world. Its foul stenches and fragrant scents will make your nostrils flare.

The medieval period spanned the years from about 1000 to 1500. For the rich and powerful it was a busy time, with lots of bloody battles, crippling crusades, and jolly jousts. It was tough on the poor peasants. Their lords built great castles within a stone's throw of their stinking hovels, then made them work like slaves. Beautiful cathedrals and holy monasteries flourished, but so did the plague. When it came down to basics, everyone suffered from the deadly medieval muck!

A black rat dies of plague.

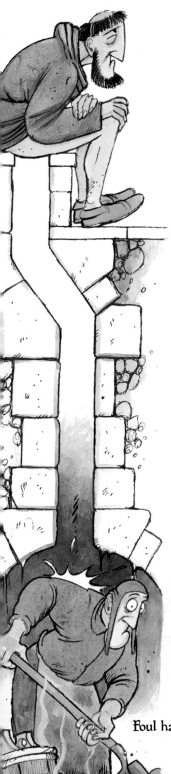

1066 and All That Rot

It's 1066 and - imagine the stench -
The English are fighting the Norman-French.
Old Harold is slain, and William is king.
Some terrible smells does his conquering bring.

The kings and queens are top of the pile,
They try to smell sweet, but are mostly quite vile.
There are Willies and Johns, Henrys and Eds,
They govern our lands and hack off our heads.

The knights and nobles have castles strong -
Don't get too close, there's a powerful pong
From the muck and manure that is thrown in the moat.
If you dare to look down you can see it all float.

We peasants are given the most rotten time,
We work in the mud and sleep in the grime.
At times we are pilgrims for a breath of fresh air.
Just give us a scratch and a sniff, if you dare.

But guess who it is who rules the rot,
And loves the filth from the chamber pot?
It's the rats and the fleas, who bring us bad luck
With death and disease in medieval muck.

The heads of enemies made good missiles!

Foul habits!

5

Peasant Pongs

Most people in medieval Europe were poor peasants. They scratched a mouldy living from the soil. They also scratched their miserable bodies – for underneath their stinky woollen garments they were riddled with fleas and lice. One medieval joker said that the smelly peasants only washed twice in their life – once when they were baptised and once before they were buried. But keeping clean was no easy matter and, sadly, many young peasants died from all sorts of lousy diseases.

Peasants had to work for their lord in return for farming their own measly plots of land.

A villein, or serf, is spreading muck on the lord's land. The lord owns everything – even the cow dung.

This mum is washing the family's rags with scraps of soap made from boiled mutton fat and wood ash. She's also bleaching dirty cloth with stale urine (it really does produce a whiter wash!).

Clogged Cities

Peasant pongs were bad enough, but imagine minding your own business in a cramped medieval city. The dirty, narrow streets are littered with hogs, dogs, rubbish and rats.

In London, 140 new shops and a double row of houses were built on London Bridge in 1176. But it's not quite as splendid as it sounds! The rotting skulls of traitors are hanging up at one end, and desperate citizens are hanging on at the other - there's only one public privy and it's not too convenient.

Your shop is littered with the refuse of everybody else's affairs — not to mention your own.

Leprosy was a rotten disease. Lepers carried bells to warn people of their presence.

If you notice a nasty squelching smell, take a look at your clogged feet. But if you fancy a breath of fresh air, don't look up!

Gong-fermours and rakers remove mundungus heaps and laystalls. Not too sure what these are? **Scratch and sniff this pile of medieval muck to find out!**

9

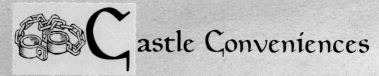

Castle Conveniences

In times of war and peace, castles provided strong homes where nobles and soldiers could shelter from their enemies or launch attacks. Castles were conveniently designed to be offensive as well as defensive. Take a look inside this besieged castle. It is packed with people and animals. They have been under siege for several weeks - so there's plenty in here to cause offence!

The moat has the most obnoxious odour – these guards are desperate to be relieved.

The thick stone walls may withstand the battering rams, but the enemy has a smellier ploy. Rotting heads of enemies and sheep are fired over the top as offensive missiles.

Prisoners are dumped in the oubliette, or secret dungeon, and conveniently forgotten!

In the Great Hall hungry nobles grab the mouldy meat before supplies run out. It's pretty rotten (there were no fridges in medieval times), but the cooks have added some extra strong spices to disguise the taste of maggots.

A spy has just been caught squatting in the garderobe. This small room was both the castle convenience and a guardroom for robes. Apparently, the smell repelled clothes moths!

oxious Knights

Tobias Lancelot, a nobleman's son, is destined to become a knight in shining armour. His main duty will be to fight for his king or lord, in return for land. Follow his story to learn the grim reality of chivalry.

1 Tobias's long training starts at the age of 7. It's quite simple once he gets the hang of it.

2 When he's 14, he serves Sir Gulliver as a squire. He learns how to ride, fight and use weapons, and to behave in a chivalrous manner – and that means no mucking about at the dinner table.

3 At last, the time comes for the final ceremony. Tobias is washed in a cold bath. After a night praying in the chapel, he becomes a Knight of the Bath.

4 Now he can have some good clean fun, with jolly events like jousting and mock battles called tournaments!

5 But the real thing is horribly bloody. In 1415 Tobias follows Henry V of England to fight the French at the Battle of Agincourt. The French get bogged down in the mud and are defeated by the much smaller English army. The stench is too much for Tobias. He squirms in agony with a nasty disease called dysentery, a foul and filthy end for a noble knight.

The war between the French and the English rumbled on for so long (1337–1453), it was known as the Hundred Years' War.

Spice and Lice

The countries of medieval Europe were ruled by a lot of mouldy monarchs. But above them, and even more powerful, was the Christian Church. In 1095 the Pope, head of that Church, heard that the Turkish Muslims had taken over the Holy Land and wouldn't let in the Christians. Bands of peasants, knights and even children went crusading off to rescue the Holy Land. In 1099, after a bloody massacre, the Christians captured Jerusalem. But seven crusades and two centuries later it was back in the hands of the Muslims.

The crusaders picked up all sorts of exotic things in the east. Some, like scented spice and Turkish baths, were real delights. Others, like leprosy and lice, were not so nice.

According to one foul story, the crusaders ate the massacred Turks.

Love-In-Mist was very popular with the Crusaders. They crushed the seeds and dusted the powder into their hair to drive out lice.

Crusaders weren't the only folk to fancy a bit of spice. In the late 15th century, explorers like Bartholomew Diaz and Vasco da Gama from Portugal went in search of the spice islands of the East Indies. A shipload of spice was worth a small fortune! It was the perfect way to disguise rotten medieval food. One famous Spanish explorer, Christopher Columbus, sailed west instead of east, and in 1492 landed up off the coast of America. These are his ships.

One of the great explorers of the Middle Ages was a Venetian called Marco Polo — it took him four years to travel to China and the aromatic east.

Filthy Facts

Pollution solutions

The stench of medieval muck did not go unnoticed! In London, strict laws were passed to stop people causing offence:

1 Butchers were not allowed to sell rotten meat — except to strangers.

2 Pigs were not allowed to roam the streets — if you came across a stray pig you could cut its throat and take its carcass.
The owner could try and buy the dead pig off you for one penny per foot.

3 Anyone caught polluting the city with coal-smoke could be executed.

4 Bakers selling mouldy loaves could be dragged through the streets tied to the back of a cart.

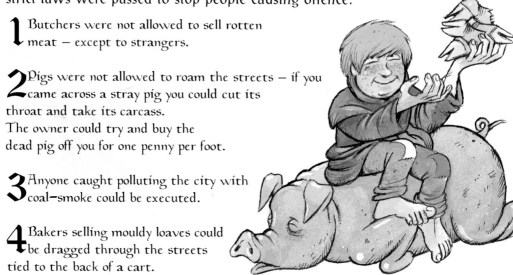

Doctors' diagnosis

Doctors who thought they could diagnose deadly diseases by examining a patient's urine were known as 'piss-prophets'. Some people tricked the doctor by substituting a jar of animal wee.

Mucking about

Football in medieval times was really foul – it was played with a pig's bladder. There were no rules and no ref. In 1314 Edward II of England was a real spoilsport – he banned football in London on the grounds that it was too mucky.

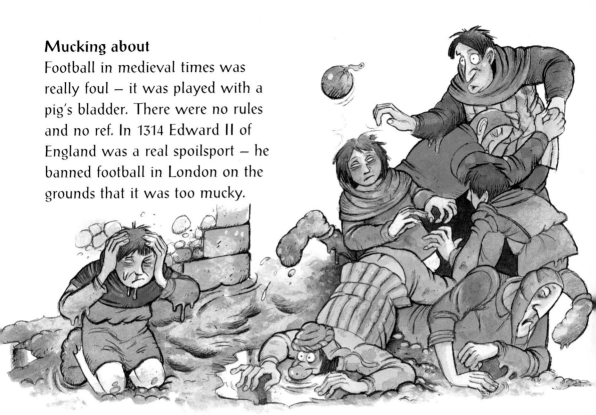

Sometimes the pressure of mucking about got too much. In 1184 Emperor Frederick and his German knights were having a merry time in their castle garderobe when the floor collapsed. They fell 12 metres into the cesspit below, and came to a sticky end!

Saintly Smells

The most heavenly smells wafted forth from the monasteries and convents. Monks and nuns washed at least several times a year, and filled their silent days with the sweet odours of herbs and incense. They cared dutifully for the sick and poor, but their own habits may seem rather strange to us.

These monks are queuing up in the 'bloodletting-house' for their monthly bleeding session. To the soothing sound of psalms, the barber-surgeon removes their top-knots (tonsures) and then takes a pint of blood.

Stale urine is collected and stored in huge vats. It is sold to cloth-makers and leather-workers.

Not all priests had a peaceful time. The Archbishop Thomas Becket was murdered in Canterbury Cathedral on the eve of 29th December 1170, for opposing Henry II's plans to reduce Church power in England. As Becket's body grew cold, the vermin that were living in his layers of clothing started to crawl out. A chronicler described the grisly scene: 'the vermin boiled over like water in a simmering cauldron, and the onlookers burst into alternate weeping and laughter.' Becket became a saint and Canterbury a popular place for pilgrims.

Glorious Gardens

Medieval gardens were full of deliciously fragrant flowers and herbs. People took pride in their private plots. One lady grew over 250 different herbs in her kitchen garden. Monks also grew herbs in the large monastery gardens. In 1278 the Abbot of Puzarre was so disgusted with the smell of the fresh young novices (men who came to learn to be monks) that he created a special aromatherapy pack for them. It was so popular that soon all his monks and visitors smelled of peppermint and roses.

Scratch and sniff this monk's sweet breath!

But not all remedies were so effective. Some, like these, sound positively foul!

For rotten toothache: hang the beak of a magpie round your neck

For ye horrid headache: put stinking goat's cheese on your head

For swollen feet: boil a dog with worms and pig's marrow and rub on

For a fever: drink a mixture of hedgehog grease and dung beetles

For boils: place a poultice of pigeons' droppings on the oozing bits

For ye stomach ache: inhale odious fumes of old shoes or burning horsehair

For ye broken nose: sniff warm bull's dung

For any disorder: purchase fresh scrapings of skull from hanged criminals.

No sweet-smelling flowers could disguise the stench of blood in this operation.

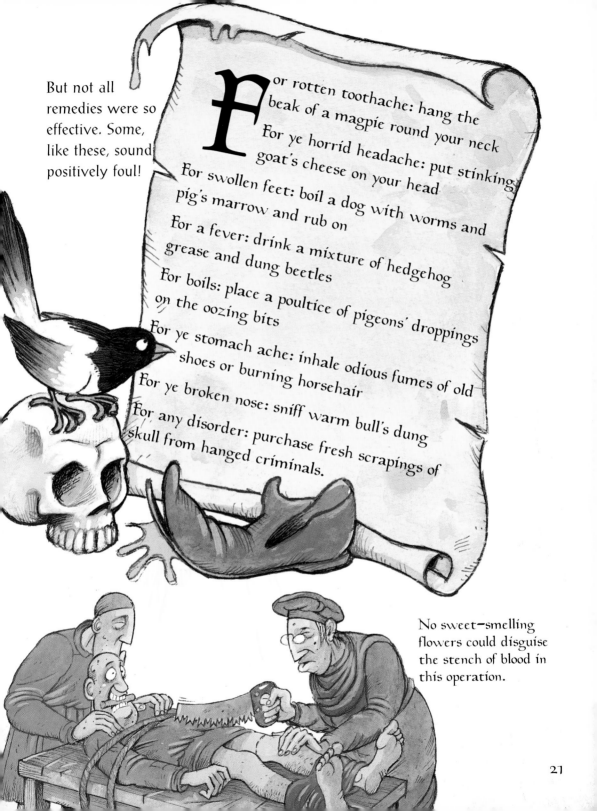

Poisonous Punishments

Criminals, traitors, witches and heretics were cruelly punished. Imagine ending up like one of these.

Terrible tortures

Pillory. This poor chap has been convicted of selling 37 putrid pigeons – he's been shackled to the pillory, with the foul stench of the pigeons burning beneath him.

Scold's bridle. Nagging wives soon lost their tongues with this device screwed on their heads.

Pilliwinks. This nasty medieval hand-crushing device put the screws on many criminals.

The Rack. The pain from this terrible ordeal stretches the imagination beyond belief.

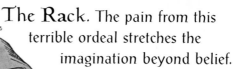

Staked out

Joan of Arc, a young French peasant, dressed up as a soldier and in 1429 helped to free the city of Orléans from the English army. She was captured and accused by the English of being a witch. She was burnt at the stake in 1431. Five hundred years later she was proclaimed a saint.

Hang it all

Some criminals were hanged, drawn and quartered. Hugh Despenser – one of Edward II's chief advisers – was slowly dispensed with. He was hanged from the gallows, then taken down while still alive to have his intestines cut out and burned before his eyes. His head ended up on London Bridge.

Juicy Jobs

There were lots of savoury and unsavoury jobs in medieval times. Fancy one of these!

Boghouse owner

Boghouse owners got filthy rich while their clients got sparkling clean. In Paris there were 32 public bathhouses, or stews. Eventually, most were shut down because they were too offensive.

Spitter and Taster

These were really juicy jobs! The spitter turned the spitting pig and the taster checked to see whether it was poisoned before the lord took a bite. In the end it was often the taster who did the spitting!

Scratch and sniff for a rotten reminder of medieval meals.

Gong-fermour

William Mokkyng and Nicholas Richeandgood are the gong-fermours of Queenborough Castle. They earn a good wage but their job is the absolute pits.

Fool

Some people tried to make a living by acting the fool. They went about telling dirty jokes, and doing crazy things like waving pigs' bladders under children's noses.

Tooth-drawer

This job needs little artistic skill. Just turn up at the weekly market and yank out a few mouthfuls of rotten teeth. The stench is a small price to pay for such a juicy job.

Castle-perfumer

Castles needed a good spring-clean from time to time. This professional castle-cleaner is pumping perfumed bellows on to the Lady's bed to freshen it up. He finishes off the job with a sprinkling of lavender and tansy to keep the fleas away.

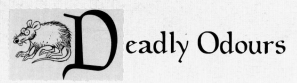eadly Odours

In the 1340s the Black Death – a foul and fatal epidemic of plague – nipped across Europe from Asia, killing one third of the entire population of Europe in a few years. Its symptoms were ghastly: stinking black buboes (sores) as large and oozing as rotten oranges, fetid breath and vile vomit. The stench of the dead thrown into huge burial pits was overpowering. Fleeing was all very well. But no-one guessed that the plague was actually spread by fleas from plague-infected rats!

Rats

The rats were having the time of their life —
Muckheaps were high and stenches were rife —
When all of a sudden, from out of the rot
A plague popped up and zapped the lot.
Their fleas jumped off and left the mud
To try a taste of human blood.
They took one slurp and drank their fill,
And after that began to kill.
They spread the plague with each small suck —
Revenge for medieval muck!

How to avoid ye plague

1. Stick your head under a toilet
2. Eat a mixture of treacle and chopped-up snakes that have been dead for 10 years
3. Strap the scrapings of a chicken's bottom onto your sores
4. Stuff sweet-smelling flowers up your nose and wash your mouth in vinegar
5. Flee as fast and far as possible

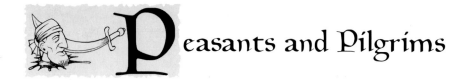

Peasants and Pilgrims

Millions were killed in the Black Death, leaving the countryside haunted with 'ghost-villages'. In England the survivors were still reeling from the shock when the government ordered everyone to pay an extra tax. The poor peasants had always been a bit revolting, but this was more than they could stomach.

In 1381 Wat Tyler and John Ball led thousands of rebellious peasants to confront the 14-year-old king, Richard II, in London. At first, the young king promised them more freedom. Then he did the dirty on them. Tyler and Ball were bumped off and the peasants were left headless. They disbanded and went home.

The Peasants' Revolt or the revolting peasants?

Some people went on pilgrimages to escape their odorous life. This riotous rabble are off to Canterbury to visit the shrine of Thomas Becket. They're spending the night in a flea-ridden tavern, listening to the miller's rude tale. *The Canterbury Tales* were written by Geoffrey Chaucer in the 14th century. They tell us just how revolting life in medieval times could be.

Scratch and sniff for the full effect of this teeming tavern.

29

Pungent Puzzles

Hangman

What is brown, slimy, stinks and is an
old-fashioned word for medieval muck?   _ _ _ _ _ _ _ _ _ _

When you've worked it out, challenge a friend to a game of
hangman.

Medieval mindbogglers

1 Was pilliwinks a) a medieval game using counters b) a form of
torture c) a medieval method of greeting by winking?

2 In the Middle Ages doctors would examine a patient's wee to say
what was wrong with them. What else was urine used for?

3 A rat bite was the cause of the plague. True or false?

A lousy choice

In Sweden, choosing a mayor
was a really lousy affair.
Anyone who fancied the
position sat round a table with
his beard resting on the edge.
A louse was placed in the
middle of the table and the
man whose beard it crawled
onto first was elected mayor.
See if you can find which
beard the louse in the centre of
this puzzle will tickle first!

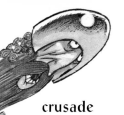

Glossary

crusade	a holy war fought by Christians for their religion
cesspit	a deep pit containing the contents of a toilet
chivalry	the rules for how a knight should fight bravely and fairly and behave towards ladies
dysentery	a horrible disease that causes diarrhoea
epidemic	a disease that spreads rapidly over large areas
flagellant	a person who whips themself to say sorry for their sins
garderobe	a loo in a castle, also used as a wardrobe to store clothes
gong-fermour	someone who empties medieval cesspits
hovel	a poor peasant's home
jousting	a combat between two knights on horseback, with lances
laystall	a pile of muck or rubbish
leprosy	a disease that causes terrible sores on the skin
moat	a wide ditch filled with water, surrounding and protecting a castle
mundungus	a medieval word for muck
plague	a foul disease spread by rat fleas
reredorter	the toilet in a monastery
serf	a peasant who serves the lord by working his land
siege	when a castle is surrounded by the enemy, trapping the people inside
squire	a boy who serves a knight
tonsure	the top of a monk's head which is shaved
tournament	a competition between knights on horseback
villein	a peasant who serves the lord by working his land

Index